Work, Neighbors, and Ship Disasters

Work, Neighbors, and Ship Disasters

Poems by

John David Muth

© 2025 John David Muth. All rights reserved.
This material may not be reproduced in any form, published,
reprinted, recorded, performed, broadcast,
rewritten or redistributed without
the explicit permission of John David Muth.
All such actions are strictly prohibited by law.

Cover design by Shay Culligan
Cover image *Titanic Sinking* by Willie Stoewer (1912)

ISBN: 978-1-63980-961-5
Library of Congress Control Number: 2025950935

Kelsay Books
502 South 1040 East, A-119
American Fork, Utah 84003
Kelsaybooks.com

To former colleagues who became lifelong friends

Dan, Bob, and Keith

Acknowledgments

Thank you to the following publications, in which versions of these poems previously appeared:

Inevitable Carbon (Kelsay Books, 2017): "Lies Hurt Less"

Misfit Magazine: "Hillbilly Stew," "Dodge the Guillotine," "The Horseman Comes," "I Don't Like My Colleagues Very Much"

U.S. 1 Worksheets: "Suttee for a Teddy Bear," "Sweet Seed," "Vultures"

Verse-Virtual: "Observing Immolation," "Hummel Massacre," "My Favorite Sweater"

*The people and events depicted within this collection are fictional.
Any similarity between these poems and reality
is entirely coincidental
and amusingly tragic.*

Contents

Part I: Dean Syphilis

Sailing on the *Britannic*	17
A Message from the Provost's Office	19
Escape the *Hindenburg*	20
No Department Is Truly Safe	22
Dean Syphilis vs. Devil Duck	24
The Dangers of AI and AEI	26
Director of University Human Resources	28
Twenty Years on the Job	30
Scratch a Cynic	32
My Identity Is an Analogy	34
Bolero at Rush Hour	36

Part II: Mr. Eindhoven's Neighborhood

Vultures	41
My Neighbor Describes Her Sleeve Tattoo	43
Dumpster Socks	45
Lonely Woodpecker	47
Dead End Neighbor	48
Living with Bugs	49
Observing Immolation	51
Why Does Sheila Hate Me?	52
The Horseman Comes	54
Hummel Massacre	56
Slug Porn	58
My Fifth Pound Cake	60

Part III: Working from Home

Virtual Advising from Home 65
Eulogy for a Tube TV 67
Jilted on the *Titanic* 68
Hillbilly Stew 70
Suttee for a Teddy Bear 72
Stormtrooper Staff Meeting 74
In Memoriam 76

Part IV: Hitting the Iceberg

Lies Hurt Less 81
An Unpleasant Stay at the *Munich Hotel* 82
Sweet Seed 85
Dodge the Guillotine 86
My Favorite Sweater 88
I Don't Like My Colleagues Very Much 90
I Dream of *The Shining* 92
A Meeting with the Queen Dean 94
Interviewing for a Similar Job 96

Epilogue

Ten Percent Off Cremation 101

Part I:
Dean Syphilis

Sailing on the *Britannic*

My title is academic counselor,
though I am more of an advisor,
though I also counsel when it is needed.
This is my third job
at William Henry Harrison State University
named after a president
who gave a two-hour inaugural address
and then died after one month in office,
accomplishing almost nothing.
Our administration carries on the tradition.

Twenty years ago, I started as an assistant dean.
Two years into the job,
they reorganized the department.
They then made me a program coordinator.
This position lasted for five years,
until budget cuts were enacted
due to low student enrollment.
I was laid off but despite my best wishes,
no other college was hiring,
and it was back to my abusive orphanage.
I have been in my current position
for the last thirteen years.

I always expect the hammer to fall a third time.
My wariness has not faded with the years.

In my office hangs a picture
of Violet Constance Jessup,

a stewardess who suffered
three mishaps during her career:

the collision of the *Olympic* in 1911
the sinking of the *Titanic* in 1912
and the sinking of the *Britannic* in 1916.
My colleagues think she is an ancestor,
but she is really an icon of endurance,
proof it is possible to survive
three failures in the same profession.

A Message from the Provost's Office

I scan a conga line of work e-mails
consisting of angry students
and self-congratulating faculty.
There is also a new announcement:
we're getting a new boss:
an assistant executive associate dean.

His picture reveals
a badly molded statue
of petrified cream cheese
in a nondescript, dark gray suit.
He smiles with his thumb up,
the best way of telling the world
he has not been self-aware since 1982.

My eyes fall on one of his several quotes:
I believe in giving students,
regardless of their background,
the opportunity for personal empowerment.
I hope he feels the same way about his staff.

I look up his name online,
notice he had a bit of trouble
at his last university. Three female students
graduated with substandard GPA's
after private consultations with him.
Coincidentally, his wife filed for divorce.
Subsequently, he left for health reasons.
I wonder if HR did any research on this guy
before offering him a six-figure job.
Of course they didn't.

Escape the *Hindenburg*

Working at a university today
is like being a crewman
on the *Hindenburg Zeppelin*.
It looks majestic on the outside
but one off-putting word
misinterpreted phrase
or miscommunication of intention,
and a spark ignites the hydrogen.

A student came to my office during registration,
said her parents pay a lot of money for tuition.
It was my job to make a class schedule
that would not give her anxiety.
When she asked me what I recommended,
I replied a Xanex and some manners.

An hour later,
I am being chastised by a boss
who lectures me about customer service
and how hard the Pandemic has been
for younger people.

I'd like to suggest
these younger people
spend a week in a bombed-out Ukrainian city.
They could then speak about hardship.
Instead, I imagine
jumping from the window
sliding down a mooring rope
and running from the tarmac
to a different occupation,

just before the blackened skeleton
of this once nearly tolerable place to work
crashes to the ground.

No Department Is Truly Safe

Almost everything in my office is white:
the thin sheet rock walls,
the three bookshelves that have
almost nothing on them,
and the drop ceiling
low enough for me to hit my head
if I jumped high enough.

This white is not the purity
associated with Western culture.
The mourning of Chinese belief
seems more appropriate.
I have been here for thirteen years,
another layer of bad luck for me.
At least I can work from home
two days per week.

Alice, a co-worker of ten years,
and fellow *Titanic* enthusiast,
passes by my door
holding a cardboard box.
Tomorrow, she starts a new job.
She is the third person from our office
to leave this month.

The first day the new boss started,
she said she could feel the iceberg
scrape along the hull.
It wouldn't be long till this ship sank.
Three months later, she is transferring
to a new department.

She visits me before she leaves
and asks if I found room on a lifeboat.
I tell her there is a program coordinator position
at the School of Engineering.
Maybe I'll get an interview.

We promise to keep in touch.
I wish her good luck on the *Carpathia*
not wanting to mention
the ship that rescued the *Titanic* survivors
was itself sunk six years later.

Dean Syphilis vs. Devil Duck

Our first interaction was pleasant.
He asked about our aspirations and hobbies
career goals and suggestions for improvement.
We didn't even know we were infected.

Then, came the chancre:
sporadic calls and texts on the weekend,
getting a sycophant to spy
on our lunchroom conversations.

The crazy crept in later:
threatening to reprimand us
for leaving a few minutes early,
adding on duties
meant for a higher-paid position.

My co-workers,
friends who were here for years,
left for other positions.
I'm one of the last ones now.

I send out resumes but get few interviews.
Maybe they want to pay
a younger person less money.
Maybe my reputation precedes itself.

My first boss said my personality
was like escargot,
you needed an open mind to try it
and an exotic pallet to really like it.
Such honesty is rare in academia.

Dean Syphilis watches me
from the office kitchen
checking to see if I am working.
I keep my eyes on my computer,
pick up a rubber duck,
black with devil horns,
a gag gift from my best friend,
and begin squeezing it methodically.

Devil Duck is able to make
Dean Syphilis disappear,
but like the symptoms
of a serious venereal disease,
he'll be back eventually.

The Dangers of AI and AEI

We sit in a small auditorium
listening to an academic coordinator
instruct us about artificial intelligence,
how students are using it
to write research papers and take exams
and how we as advisors
can remind them about its misuse
and help faculty instructors
maintain academic integrity.

My boss sits in the front row,
arms folded and legs crossed.
He gives a passive-aggressive mention
that AI may one day be used
to do academic advising,
rendering our jobs obsolete.

Feeling annoyed by his unnecessary response,
I reply if they learned to put
emotional intelligence into one of these AI systems,
we would have no need for bosses.

It would be refreshing to be led by something
that recognized the value of a productive staff
did not hold grudges
and did not focus on its own ego and ambition.

That was well worth the written reprimand.

Director of University Human Resources

I nicknamed her Grendel,
as she is a monster out of legend,
hideous and deformed:
double-knit pant suits
too much make-up,
the child of an even greater demon:
the Queen Dean herself.

She crosses the threshold of my office,
recoils at the sight
of a Celtic cross tapestry
that hangs on my wall.

Trying not to look at the cross,
yellow coffee teeth snarling,
she informs me I have yet to complete
my modules on avoiding sexual harassment.
They are due next Tuesday.
Failure to complete them on time
will result in a reprimand.

Red stiletto fingernails splay out,
awaiting my response.
Undaunted,
I look into her dead, black opal eyes
and inform her they will be done this week.
She nods and turns to leave,
pausing a moment
to mention her regret
we won't be getting our raise this year.
Citing fiscal austerity due to the economy,
she flashes a diamond ring and laughs.

Twenty Years on the Job

I sit in the staff cafeteria,
listening to one of the University's
seventy-five vice-presidents
talk about dedication.
Several dozen employees
sit at round tables in groups of two or three.
Most are not paying attention.

School employees are invited to this luncheon
after each completed decade of service.
They get a plaque and a gift of appreciation.
Ten years ago,
I received chicken marsala and an umbrella
with the University's logo.
For my twentieth year,
they are serving pulled pork sandwiches.

I stare at my twenty-year gift:
a brass paperweight with the University's logo,
and think about a Roman legionary
who could retire after twenty-five years
with fourteen years pay
and the respect of his fellow citizens.

I could never retire in twenty-five years,
and respect is as elusive

as a hot girl in high school
who laughs when you ask her out.

The overweight man next to me
eats his sandwich like he is about to be attacked.
I think he works in the registrar's office,
but I cannot remember his name.

I ask him how long he's been at the University.
Without looking at me
he responds thirty years.
There is no gift near him,
and I ask what an employee gets
for thirty years of service.

He tells me hypertension.

Scratch a Cynic

Jess and Carlos were students of mine
when I started my advising career.
Twice a year, we meet for dinner.

Jess is a physician's assistant
who just bought her own home.
Carlos is a financial planner,
married and expecting his first child.

They were freshmen when we met,
twenty years ago,
bright, young and eager,
the first in their families to go to college.
I was the older version of them,
ready to mentor and inspire.
Education was my sword
in the fight to make the world better.

Jess asks me about work,
smiling, knowing she just lit the fuse.
They both know I'm jaded now,
but we're close enough friends
for my rants to be endearing.

I talk about students who cry from anxiety,
because they can't decide on an art class,

parents who use the term *mental health issues*
to exonerate their children
from cheating on exams or failing classes.

I talk about idiots with Ph.D.'s
who rule their departments like petty kingdoms
bend rules to suit their needs
treat their staff like servants.

Carlos raises his glass,
wishes me an early retirement.
Our glasses clink together,
and I feel both happiness
my former students turned out so well
and sad how my experiences
all but extinguished the spark in me.

My Identity Is an Analogy

He comes into my office
for an advising session,
thin and gangly,
dressed in black.

On my records,
it says his name is David,
but he calls himself Itchy,
identifies as a spider,
sometimes as a badger.

When he asks my identity,
I bow my head.
It's been a long week,
and he is my last Friday appointment.

I tell him I identify
as one of the butchers on the *Lusitania*.
When the ship started to sink,
these men crowded into an elevator
to escape from the rising water.
As the elevator ascended,
the power failed.
Trapped between decks,
they could not get out
and eventually drowned.

That is my identity:
a middle-aged man trapped in a job
living in a damaged country,
watching both of us sink to our demise.

He looks at me disgusted,
tells me meat is murder.
I respond that my other identity
is a can of Raid,
and he quickly leaves the room.

Bolero at Rush Hour

Stuck in traffic on the way home from work,
Ravel's *Bolero* comes on the radio.
I heard it with my grandmother
nearly thirty years ago,
and remembered how she smiled when I mentioned
she was only eight-years-old
when it was composed.

She's been gone now
for over twenty-five years,
but *Bolero* still sounds the same.

The floor of her foyer creaks
while a snare drum softly patters.
I smell her pancakes
as the English horn soars,
feel the scratch
of the old spare room blanket
when the saxophone sways.

Strings, winds and brass
play louder and faster.
People rage inside of their cars.
Grandmom died
mom died
COVID stepped on the pieces
of an already broken country.

My own body aches
from the weight of years.

A car horn drowns out
the sound of the final cymbal crash.
I want to go back in time
to see my grandmother's smile again,
and her gapped ivory teeth
worn down by decades of fitful sleep.

Part II:
Mr. Eindhoven's Neighborhood

Vultures

The country road that leads to my home
was never built for heavy traffic.
Deer in various stages of decay
lay in drainage ditches
like victims of a World War II death march.
One has a large hole in its hindquarters.
Another is nothing more
than a spinal cord and half a ribcage.
The township rarely cleans them up.
That job falls to our resident vultures.

They perch on top of the water tower
that overlooks this bedroom community,
usually a dozen or more,
scanning the area for road kill.
Here, the automobile and the vulture
have a symbiotic relationship.
I myself have given a squirrel or two
to their dinner menu,
unintentionally, of course.

I lie on the back deck of my condo,
watching them gently circle
a prospective meal.
It is peaceful and relaxing,
a welcome end to a stressful day.

I hate it when they liken
this hardworking creature

to a rapacious human.
Vultures eat the dead.

Rapacious humans eat the living.
Some of them are eating me right now
though the bites are too small to notice.

My Neighbor Describes Her Sleeve Tattoo

*The ivy creeping up my arm
represents my love for nature
and my middle name is also Ivy.*

*The baby footprint near my bicep
is the big brother I never had.
Three years before I was born,
mom had a miscarriage at four weeks.
I still cry about it.*

*According to ExploitYourDNA.com,
I am 4% African.
The chains around my forearm
represent the suffering of my people.
Being brought up white in New Hampshire,
I kinda always felt out of place.*

*The bleeding dagger by my shoulder
stands for all of the men I dated
who broke my heart.
The skull on the tricep
reminds me that death is imminent.*

I look across the street
while she continues to talk
and notice another neighbor
texting on his phone while he walks his dog,
oblivious to his surroundings.

The little brown terrier

patters up to an azalea bush
lifts its leg and urinates
and though unpleasant,
the scene is far more endurable
than this one-sided conversation.

Dumpster Socks

Burning cow shit
filters through my nose hair
as I open the door to my second story deck.

Looking down, I see our
across-the-street neighbor
sitting on a folding chair
smoking a cigar.
His wife won't allow him
to smoke near their condo,
so he comes here to impart his fumes.

I often see him walk to the garbage shed
in his stocking feet.
It makes me shiver
to see him stand among the bags
and discarded appliances,
imagine the filth he brings into his home.

He looks up at me
says hello
then asks how my Aunt Mary is doing.
I told him she was ill six years ago.
She died a year later.
I let him know,
but he still kept asking how she was.

I now tell him she's fine.
He gives a thumbs up and crosses his leg

rests his right ankle on his left knee.
A label from a soup can
sticks to the bottom
of his blackened sock.

Lonely Woodpecker

I hear a patter on the side of the house,
like a child's toy machine gun
firing from a distance,
or a Jehovah's Witness
high on methamphetamines
rapidly knocking on a neighbor's door,
ready to explain
how crank is God and God is crank.

Outside, there is a woodpecker
making a coaster-sized hole
in the vent leading to my attic.
He visits every afternoon.
Every afternoon, I throw an acorn at him.
He flies away
only to return the next day.

A thousand trees dot my neighborhood,
but he wants to peck holes in my house.
Maybe he's lonely.
There is a squirrel living in my attic.
I hear her skittering in the early morning.
Perhaps he cannot find
a female of his own species
and wants to date her.
It would not surprise me.
He is an asshole.
If I was a female woodpecker,
I wouldn't want to date him either.

Dead End Neighbor

He lives at the far side of our street
near a dead end,
which is an appropriate location
for this rotund and balding man-boy.

His hobbies include
drag racing down our road
in a 1988 Oldsmobile
playing country music loudly
with all his windows open
and inviting his girlfriend over
for drunken shouting matches on the weekend.

We often hear his car alarm at night:
the shrieks of a hitchhiker,
who once majored in modern opera,
being murdered by a sadist.

I call the police
for the fourth time this month,
wondering why he would need an alarm
for a car more brown than white from rust.
It's like putting a chastity belt
on a ninety-year-old nun:
too much protection
for what no one wants.

Living with Bugs

There is a light red blotch on the ceiling:
the remains of two mosquitoes.
I think they were mating
when my magazine hit its mark.
At least they died in the sack.
It's the way I always wanted to go.

Spiders spin their webs
in the corners of my foyer
waiting for something
to crawl under the front door.

A black ant dashes across my carpet:
another scout for his tribe.
He escapes under the home entertainment center
before I can get him.
I've killed four of them
within the last few days.
Their bards sing songs about my wife,
the auburn giant who spills
oceans of raw sugar
on the kitchen floor every morning
when she makes her coffee.

The auburn giant bellows.
I run to the spare room
to see her pointing to a stink bug
resting on the window sill.
I pick it up with a tissue

intending to crush it,
but my wife reminds me of the smell,

and I imagine
an old man's laundry basket
sitting in a damp basement.

I take the lucky bug downstairs
and toss him into the grass.

Observing Immolation

Flipping through TV channels
on a weekday evening,
a gray, grainy ship appears on the screen,
badly damaged
half-covered in smoke.

This is a documentary
about the *SS Morrow Castle,*
a luxury ship that made runs to Havana
during the Great Depression
to circumvent Prohibition.

In 1934, the ship caught fire.
Most of the officers and crew
abandoned their posts and escaped,
leaving passengers:
directionless,
half-drunk on Cuban Rum,
to die screaming in the flames.

The narrator's descriptions
agitate my wife.
She asks if we can watch
something less macabre.
I switch to a news station
where experts are debating
who will win the next presidential election.

Why Does Sheila Hate Me?

My neighbor lifts weights every morning
on her front walkway,
in the same green tank top
and black spandex shorts.
She greets every passerby
with a smile and a hello,
except for me.

Those dumbbells look heavy,
maybe thirty-five pounds.
She purses her lips,
looks at the weight with visible intensity
as she moves it up and down.

She's lived two doors down from me
for nearly twenty years,
but we never got along.
One evening,
while checking my mailbox,
she approached me,
breath reeking of vodka and whey protein,
told me the women she dates
have bigger balls than me.
I told her this did not come as a surprise.
We never spoke again.

I walk over to my car.
She spots me,
scans the length of my body,
top to bottom,
like an airport X-ray machine,
blows a puff of air from her lips.

Driving past her,
I give the car horn a long honk.
An outraged grunt
follows the bang of iron on concrete.
I wish the weight had landed on her foot.

The Horseman Comes

I see him in my rearview mirror,
eyes hidden by sunglasses
lips twisted in anger
riding my back bumper
though I am going the speed limit.

At first, I wonder if he's drunk,
late for a weekend job,
or a victim of Irritable Bowel Syndrome.
The insignia on his front grill
comes into view:
a row of four interconnected circles,
and I finally understand.

His vehicle is from the Book of Revelation,
one of the four horsemen of shitty driving:
Audi, Mercedes, BMW, Tesla,
symbols of status to some,
a warning to others:
asshole on board.
There is no one to stop them.
Even the police no longer care.

I swerve to the shoulder of the road
and jam on the brakes.
A rush of air from the passing car
screams in my ear.
Seven trumpets blare,
meld into the sound of a horn,
as the Evil One
now rides the ass
of the Toyota that was in front of me.

Hummel Massacre

I wish my mother had collected
gold Krugerrands
instead of Precious Moments Figurines
or Apple stock
instead of Hallmark Christmas Ornaments.

She's been gone for six years,
but the attic is still brimming
with all the items a Boomer thought
would be worth money one day:
Beanie Babies in individual plastic cylinders,
collector plates of Julie Andrews movie characters
from the Franklin Mint,
TV guides in plastic covers commemorating
the last episodes of *M*A*S*H* and *Seinfeld.*

I look at the curio cabinet,
peer at the rows of figurines:
chubby-cheeked German children
skipping to school
or climbing up trees.
My parents' generation worshipped Hummels,
saw them as icons of increasing value.
They don't seem to understand
those of us born after 1960 don't care.

I turn my head,
see my father eyeing me like a sentinel.
He knows what I want to do
but will not allow it.

Eyes locked in silent combat,
I inform him telepathically
he won this battle,
but forty-eight hours after his pulse stops,
these walls will ring
with the sound of shattering porcelain.

Slug Porn

I am sitting on my couch,
watching TV on a Sunday afternoon
when I hear my cell phone ping.

An image from my door camera appears.
A pot-bellied man
with a baseball cap
stands there drinking a beer.
He is looking right at the camera,
but he does not ring the doorbell.

Bill is my neighbor.
He's a computer programmer
who moved into the neighborhood
a year after me.

I go down the stairs,
hoping he has no reason
to shoot or stab me.
We always got along,
but he divorced last year
and COVID has made everyone
a potential basket case.

Exiting the house with trepidation,
I ask Bill if he is ok.
He points the neck of the beer bottle
in the direction of the camera.
Right above the lens,
two slugs are locked
in what looks like a tedious mating ritual.

Bill sighs:
Jenny and I made love every Sunday afternoon.

I quietly nod
and go back into the house.

My Fifth Pound Cake

Sid and Mary are an elderly couple
who live three doors down from us.
They never had children,
so we feel some kinship with them.

Mary falls pretty regularly,
and they call me when they need help.
Tonight, she is lying on the bathroom floor,
tells me her legs gave out
while washing her hands.

She calls me Jack.
Sid calls me Jerry.
My real name is Jon, but I never correct them.
It's close enough for me.

Carrying her to bed is not possible.
She's a bit heavier than me,
but I have a ritual to get the job done.
I drag her to the bedroom
as gently as I can,
put her in a sitting position,
lift her by the armpits
and put her on my lap,
as I sit on the edge of the bed.

We then lie back and rotate,
until she is reclining on me like a mattress.
I then slither out from under her.
We've done this five times in the last two months.

Mary thanks me profusely and closes her eyes.
Sid takes me to the kitchen,
opens the freezer and gives me a pound cake.
Every time I help her, he gives me one.
There are four of them in my freezer now.
Walking back home,
I think about infirmity and helplessness
and wonder if Emily and I,
childless and with little family,
will face the same problems when we are old.

Part III:
Working from Home

Virtual Advising from Home

I am a slug drying on the kitchen floor,
a beached seal with shredded flippers
that cannot return to the ocean.
I came here to make some coffee
but got dizzy and dropped to the floor,
like a tightly-corseted southern belle
in a Civil War-era movie.

My work computer
ping, ping, pings
from the next room.
It's 6:00 p.m.
Ten hours and the little bastards
are still e-mailing me:
*What classes should I take
three semesters from now?
Why isn't my laptop camera working?
Can I take calculus
even though I failed elementary algebra?*

It would be a pleasure
to melt through the cracks in the floorboards,
drip into my downstairs neighbor's living room,
re-solidify on her couch,
watch a little *Jeopardy*.

I smell her dinner through the air vents.
She's making chicken stew,
probably playing with her three cats

while the Prozac pulsing through her veins
keeps out all thoughts of worry.

My wife asks me what I want for dinner.
I say chicken stew.
She wants to make vegan burgers,
and it's clear to me now
being prostrated on this floor
will be the highlight of my day.

Eulogy for a Tube TV

My tube TV died three days ago
at the age of twenty-one
in the middle of a laxative commercial.
I cannot say I blame it.

It was with me for most of my bachelorhood
watched me sleep on the couch
on innumerable dateless weekends
consoled me when a good woman got away,
or far more often,
helped me celebrate when a bad one left.
When it closed its eye for good,
my wife was there with me.
Maybe knowing I was now ok
gave it a sense of peace.

That three-hundred-pound square
of wires, glass and plastic
was the best inorganic friend I ever had.
If Buddhist reincarnation
also applies to electronics,
I hope they recycle it
into a defibrillator,
or a machine that delivers chemotherapy
to children with leukemia,
so it can be there for another
when their need is greatest.

Jilted on the *Titanic*

Watching TV on my sister's couch,
my niece sits next to me
puts her head on my shoulder.

When I ask if she is ok,
she tells me her boyfriend
broke up with her yesterday:
two weeks before the junior prom.
He found somebody else.

Trying to keep her from crying,
I point to the TV screen.
A documentary is reenacting
passengers on the *Titanic*
trying to escape from the sinking ship.

I tell her to imagine it's 1912.
She and her boyfriend
are passengers on the *Titanic*.
During the voyage, he leaves her
for a woman who wears her skirt
an inch above the ankle:
a real strumpet.
The ship hits an iceberg shortly after.

Being a lady of quality,
my niece gets priority for a lifeboat,
while he, a young man in the
Edwardian Age,
has to stay with the sinking ship.

He is dejected,
watching his former girlfriend
being lowered to safety
while the band plays
Nearer my God to Thee.
My niece asks if it would be proper
for her to flip him the bird
as her boat rows away.
I respond it is acceptable,
as long as she covers her smile with a fan.

Hillbilly Stew

A squirrel moved into our attic.
I hear her
skittering in the early morning.
The sound is like a rat sex orgy
sporadically disturbed by a stalking cat.

I named her Linda
after my first college girlfriend,
a nervous and chatty person.
We dated for two years.
She broke up with me
over the phone
very unexpectedly
during her study abroad semester in Belgium.
It was a collect call,
so in addition to losing a girlfriend,
I had an eighty-dollar phone bill.

Working in my home office,
I hear her scratching the floorboards above.
She is probably nesting in the insulation
eating the electric wiring
shitting all over our boxes and bags.

I look up at the ceiling
call her a little bitch
tell her pest control is coming tomorrow
to make a hillbilly stew out of her.

My eyes fall back to the computer monitor.
The student I have been advising remotely
looks at me in horror.
I apologize
blame cabin fever
and far too much caffeine.

Suttee for a Teddy Bear

He is only one year younger,
fifty to be exact,
but there is not a mark on him,
not a tear
not a loose eye
not an unraveled stitch.

His preserved looks
were not from my aloofness.
I hugged him with an earnestness
I rarely gave a woman,
and an innocence so distant in the past,
I cannot remember it.

Who will take care of my friend
when I am gone?
Maybe my wife will keep it,
until it's her time to go.
She might give it to a child
who would likely tear the ancient fabric
with self-entitled hands
and eventually cast it aside
in favor of a smart phone.

It's best he come with me,
secure within the crook of my arm
as a fire turns us both to ashes.
I doubt he'll mind cremation.
There isn't much work for an old teddy bear,
and we might get lonely in the afterlife.

I really should not drink this early in the day.

Stormtrooper Staff Meeting

My boss scheduled a virtual staff meeting
for 10:00 a.m. today,
but I have to take my father to the doctor.
Neither event can be postponed or missed.

A four-foot talking *Star Wars* Stormtrooper
stands in a corner of my home office.
I sit the action figure on my chair
in front of the computer camera
and open the window behind him.
The sun shines through,
obscuring his features.
My colleagues might be too bored to notice.
My boss couldn't find his genitals
if a hooker was holding them.

When the meeting begins,
I race to the front door
jump in the car
pick up my father
drive him to the doctor
listen to him bitch about his prostate
listen to him bitch about his acid reflux
get him to the office
wait for him to be called
wait for him to get out

drive him back to his house
listen to him bitch about the neighbors
drop him off
and get back home.

The meeting is over by the time I return.
There is an e-mail from the boss
waiting for me.

I click it on,
expecting to be reprimanded.
My boss tells me
he likes what I said
about creating a first order
but was unsure what I meant
by crushing the resistance.
He wants to discuss my strategies next week.

In Memoriam

I had a dream
a student facing academic dismissal
was crying in my office.
His parents stood between him,
their heads bowed in sorrow.
He said he has PTSD.
It came on him early last semester.
Now, he cannot eat or sleep,
all of his classes are F's.

I asked him the cause,
and he responded a calculus exam
triggered a flood of painful memories:
the loss of his foreskin almost twenty years ago.
His father wept,
cursing the day he let the doctor
mutilate his son.

I gave him my condolences,
told him mine was lost in 1972,
a year before the Paris Peace Accords
ended the Vietnam War.
I miss it sometimes,
especially when walking naked
into a cold room.

He asked to appeal his dismissal,
and I replied two semesters with a 0.0 GPA
made this impossible,
even for circumcision survivors.

His mother scowled
snapped her fingers
and my boss appeared in a puff of smoke
wearing the costume of a medieval jester.

He told me we are a student-centric office.
Like a mattress store,
the customer was always right.
He reversed the dismissal
and assured the parents
I would be attending the memorial service next week.

Part IV:
Hitting the Iceberg

Lies Hurt Less

The smartly-dressed school psychologist
tries to justify her salary,
tells us hard truths
can hurt our students' feelings
lead to depression and low self-esteem:

*Do not tell your kids
they are failing their classes.
Tell them everyone develops
in their own unique way.
Use Einstein and Edison as examples.
Never use the word dismissal.
Say they must transition to an institution
better suited to their talents.*

She asks if we have any questions,
frowns at the silence.
I tell her the workshop is enlightening.
It will make me a better advisor,
and I can't wait for this afternoon's session
about the traumatic effects
caused by micro-aggressions.

She smiles with self-satisfaction
like a coddled child,
her master's in psychology
no match for my acting skills.

An Unpleasant Stay at the *Munich Hotel*

We pull into the driveway
of an old Catskill Mansion
said to be renowned for its
authentic German ambience.

It is early afternoon,
but there is no one in reception.
A note on the desk
informs us our room number is eleven.
The key is for room twelve.

A man in a green t-shirt quickly passes,
holding a pile of towels.
He tells us in an Irish accent
the restaurant opens at 5:00.
Before I can ask if he is the manager,
he sprints up the stairs.

We walk down a long corridor.
Every room is open:
a collection of time capsules from 1975
with wood-paneled walls and avocado rugs.
Ours also has a non-working cuckoo clock
above the bed
and several chipped beer steins on the dresser.

Emily reads the hotel brochure,
while I brush my teeth.
I tell her the sewer system might be backing up.

She replies it must be the water.
The sulfur springs on the property
were used for therapy in the 1870s.

I smell the minty flatulence
coming from my toothbrush
and throw it into the trash.
Dinner inspires a nightmare:
I am an ancient Roman gladiator.
My opponent pulls my head back
but instead of slitting my throat,
he stuffs a piece of greasy Wienerschnitzel
into my mouth
and forces me to chew.

I awaken to see Emily shaking me.
She tells me there is carousing outside.
Half-empty bottles clang together.
Someone is a riding a lawnmower around the property.
She also heard the stairs creak
reminds me the lock to the door is broken.
I tell her I'll check out the noise
but drift off to sleep again.
She calls me her hero.
I think she was being sarcastic.

We get up early the next morning
splash a little fart water on our faces

and go to the reception desk.
A note from the manager
informs us they do not serve breakfast
for only two guests.
A postscript tells us to come back soon.
I write the word, *unwahrsheinlich,* underneath it.
It means *unlikely* in German,
but I am sure the owner does not know this.

Sweet Seed

She puts a bowl of pineapple in front me
suggests I eat it every day for breakfast.

Before I can inquire why,
she lists all the benefits she read about online:
It can reduce inflammation,
which is good for my arthritis.
It can aid digestion,
which might reduce my stomach gurgling.
The bromelain can also ease
the symptoms of my sinusitis.

I mention it is reputed
pineapple can sweeten
a certain bodily fluid
and suggest we do some testing,
but she pretends to ignore me
and goes out for her morning walk.

Dodge the Guillotine

We anxiously skim the pharmacy shelves
in the family planning aisle,
bypassing the condoms and vaginal lubricant
trying to find the home pregnancy tests.

Emily is a week late
her breasts hurt
she is a bit nauseous.
I share her nausea contemplating
she could be carrying another version of me.

We locate a box in the corner of the store.
Three men lie dead nearby
of self-inflicted gunshot wounds.
I guess the results were positive for them.

Racing home,
I imagine myself in Revolutionary France
lying under a guillotine blade.
The magistrate sentences me to death.
I protest my innocence
tell him I hate children
always pulled out
never lingered longer than I should.
He reminds me that sperm,
like any good army,
always sends out scouting parties
before a big attack.

Emily goes into the bathroom
a box tears
the toilet seat bangs open.
My eyes peer into the empty basket,
while the screaming crowd
throws stale bread and horse dung at me,
creating shit sandwiches
I hope I won't have to eat.

Three minutes later, she opens the door
assures me she's not pregnant.
The magistrate announces my pardon.
The crowd boos.

My Favorite Sweater

My aunt gave me this sweater,
royal blue cable-knit English wool
for my seventeenth birthday.
Thirty-four years later,
I still wear it on the bitterest
of winter days.

We are both still functional
but visibly scarred.
In my 20s, there was a slit in the back.
My mother sewed it closed.
In my 30s, the elbows wore out.
My mother sewed on patches.
In my 40s, the sleeves started to fray.
My mother was gone by then,
so my wife made the repairs.

I tell her after death
my ghost will be wearing it.
When she reaches the afterlife,
the vibrant blue color
will make me easy to find.
She jokes we're not going to the same place
and hell will be too hot for wool.

I Don't Like My Colleagues Very Much

Pick a number from a cup.
The lowest number goes first.
Take an anonymous gift from the table.
Open the wrapping
in front of your colleagues.
If the next person likes it,
they can steal it,
and you must get another gift.

Those are the rules
for our office Christmas grab bag,
an event where anticipation
resentment
and revenge
disguise themselves as holiday fun.

I hate this grab bag,
initiated by a boss who uses clichés like:
only the strong survive and
to the victor goes the spoils.
Most of my colleagues,
young and recently hired,
believe this circa-1985 stock broker philosophy.

For my gift this year,
I put a basic solar calculator,
the kind Walmart sells for $9.95,
into the box of a computer tablet
and watched with yuletide glee
as the first person unwrapped it.

My gift changed hands in quick succession.
There were looks of disappointment
barely disguised rage
and finally, the triumphal smile of Evelyn,
the office spy,
who will go home to find
a gift worthy of her treachery.

I Dream of *The Shining*

I am a fragment of Steven King's imagination,
re-interpreted by Stanley Kubrick,
bug-eyed and pale,
in a blue bathrobe and brown suede boots
standing in a locked bathroom.
A butcher's knife trembles in my hand.

The door bangs.
A chunk of wood breaks off
flies into the toilet
and lands with a plop.

Hugging the wall like a mouse,
I watch a fireman's axe
make a hole in the door
larger and larger with every strike.

Until this moment,
everything was going great.
I came to the Overlook Hotel
to get away from my job.
It offered everything I needed:
blizzards and snowdrifts,
isolation and a hedge maze.
Malevolent spirits tried to take my soul,
but they also do that at work:

deans who fetishize ambition over staff,
students who couldn't tell trauma
from inconvenience.
At least the ghosts were nice to me.

The banging stops,
and an egg-shaped head comes through
the jagged hole in the door.
It's my boss.
He tells me winter break is over.
There is a staff development workshop tomorrow.
Everyone must attend.

I start to scream.

A Meeting with the Queen Dean

A near-sighted octopus
with a bird nest wig
sits at the end of a conference table.
To her left, is a gargoyle
taking notes with a laptop.
To her right, is my boss,
wrapped in one of her tentacles
staring dreamily at the ceiling.

In an aquatic voice,
she tells us budgetary shortfalls
have now become so bad,
we need to lower our standards
to get more students.
She asks how we can do this
without compromising our program's quality.

Most of my colleagues bow their heads.
Even I am silent.

Janet,
my only remaining friend in this office,
stops her doodling
and tells the evil mollusk
it is not possible.
Employers will eventually reject
our lower quality students.

Perhaps the department can save money
by cutting our bloated management team.

A tentacle lashes out across the table,
hits Janet in the head.
She falls to the ground, unconscious.

I turn to assist her but notice she is smiling.
Her note pad depicts a rocket ship
fleeing from a burning planet
to another world, vibrant and shimmering.
She must have heard good news
from that interview she had last week.

I let my good friend sleep.
She's a mother of four
and can probably use the extra rest.

Interviewing for a Similar Job

I have been sitting at a conference table
for over forty-five minutes
while six people in business attire
throw daggers at my head:

What is your philosophy as a student counselor?
What strategies do you use to calm an angry parent?
How do you go above and beyond
to support the students in your current position?

The associate dean of the department
sits at the head of the table.
He leans forward.
Everyone turns to face him.
After a pause that reeks of B-movie drama,
he asks:

What is your definition of a boss?

It is then I know this job is not for me.
My duties will focus on pleasing him.
The people who do the work are unimportant,
just like my current job.

With all eyes on me,
I clear my throat and look at him intently:

In larger academic institutions,
a boss is like leather seats on a military vehicle:
a superfluous and impractical expenditure.
With a competent staff, they are usually not needed.

And at that moment,
I think of Engineer Jonathan Shepherd,
sitting alone in the pump room
of a sinking *Titanic,*
leg broken,
watching the water slowly rise,
resigned to his coming death,
as he waits for the bulkheads to explode.

Epilogue

Ten Percent Off Cremation

After months of searching,
I finally found a new job
outside of higher education.

I leave my old department
without a good luck party.
All of my friends are already gone,
and the younger ones are too busy
trying to climb a ladder that does not exist.

Most of the old deans left
after accusations of budget mismanagement.
They found higher positions at other universities.
My former boss is now president
of an all-female college in Massachusetts.
I'm sure he likes that a lot.
I'm sure his students do not.

Tomorrow, I start my new position
with the Division of Motor Vehicles.
Adjusting should be easy.
I am used to being an anonymous part
of a mindless bureaucracy.
At least I don't have to take work home,
and if anyone pisses me off,
I can mess up their paperwork,
make them go to the back of the line.

I drape the smallpox-infected blanket
of familiarity over my shoulders,

promise myself I'll find something more rewarding
once I get closer to age sixty-five.

Maybe I can find employment at a funeral home.
I'm used to working with people
already dead on the inside.
They might even throw in a discount
when it's time for my eternal rest.

About the Author

John David Muth was born and raised in central New Jersey. He has worked in the field of higher education for over twenty-five years. Writing, reading, hiking, and taking road trips are his favorite distractions.

Muth is a member of the Delaware Valley Poets/U.S. 1 Poet's Cooperative. His work has appeared in such journals as *Misfit Magazine, Verse-Virtual,* and *U.S. 1 Worksheets.* He is the author of seven collections of poetry: *A Love for Lavender Dragons* (Kelsay Books, 2016), *Inevitable Carbon* (Kelsay Books, 2017), *Odysseus in Absaroka* (Kelsay Books, 2018), *Reassure the Phoenix* (Kelsay Books, 2019), *Dreams of a Viking Wedding* (Kelsay Books, 2020), *Misanthropes Rarely Procreate* (Kelsay Books, 2021), and *Songs of Arthritis* (Kelsay Books, 2022).

www.ingramcontent.com/pod-product-compliance
Lightning Source LLC
Chambersburg PA
CBHW072202160426
43197CB00012B/2491